"A devotional rarely comes along that effectively bridges the gap between the great truths of Scripture and the everyday life of teenagers. This book does just that. Tom Richards presents real issues that demand real decisions with social, moral and spiritual implications for daily life. Each chapter includes provocative stories to stimulate thought and discussion questions that demand thoughtful response. Chapters conclude as the reader is asked to choose to make a commitment to live for Christ in the area he or she has just studied. This book is ideal for individual or group study and will challenge teens and young adults to incorporate the Scriptures into daily life and decisions."
Dr. Gary Benedict, President, Christian and Missionary Alliance

"Who do you suppose loves us the most? God. Who made us? God. Who established the best kind of life for us? God. Could it be that God knows more than we know and—having our best interest at heart—prescribes the best way to live...the way that brings joy to us and brings glory to Him?

"Tom Richards has given us a great gift in this book. He points out a life of freedom and joy. Freedom? Freedom of the rails. Does a train have more freedom when it is on the rails or when it is de-railed? This is a great guide for staying on track.

"I recommend this book with enthusiasm."
Dr. Bob Ricker, Retired President and CEO, Baptist General Conference

"This book is written by a young man who really understands youth, culture, and ministry. Tom Richards' writing is very straightforward; it is full of sound biblical truth, replete with fresh/current illustrations, and laced with thought-provoking discussion questions. Read it. Use it. It will greatly enhance your insight and ministry effectiveness."
Troy Dobbs, Senior Pastor, Grace Church

"Students hunger to know what the Bible says about the issues they struggle with every day. Teenagers also desperately want adults to shoot straight with them and treat them like the adults they are becoming. Tom Richards will be received and celebrated by the teenage community for doing just that! His honest look at culture and the pressures teenagers face, mixed with Scripture and practical, godly principles, have the potential to change lives and reclaim this generation for Jesus!"

Heather Flies, Junior High Pastor and Youth Communicator, Wooddale Church and Youth Specialties

DEVOTIONS
FOR REAL LIFE

summerside
PRESS

Summerside Press, Inc.
Minneapolis 55438

www.summersidepress.com

iChoose: Devotions for Real Life
Copyright 2010 © by Tom Richards

ISBN 978-1-935416-73-9

Cover and interior design by Studio Gear Box
www.studiogearbox.com
Cover photo by Lawrence Week/Shutterstock

Summerside Press™ is an inspirational publisher offering fresh, irresistible books to uplift the heart and engage the mind.

Printed in China

To my mentors, Tim and Jerenne Block,

for their faithful example of choosing to live for Christ,

and for developing my passion for ministry.

TABLE OF CONTENTS

DEVOTIONS

WEEK ONE

FOR REAL LIFE

The example I choose to set

Great choices can bring tremendous blessing, just as terrible choices can bring total disaster. Life is all about choices, and who better to make your choices than you? Between the ages of 13 and 30, you'll make some of the absolute biggest decisions of your life. In most cases, you'll live with the consequences of your decisions for the rest of your life. What's a guy or girl to do?

Every decision you ever make is shaped by what you believe about yourself and what you believe about God. Will you choose authentic relationships over hookups and phony friends? Will you be brave and choose to stand up for your faith and what you believe in? Will you choose to use your unique gifts and talents to make a difference in the world around you? Will you choose God's truth over lies from hell that will knock you down every time?

You may know what you believe about yourself and God, but sometimes it's tough to live out what you believe. *iChoose* is full of real stories of others who faced tough issues and had to choose between living for God and living for themselves. Some made fantastic choices and others made foolish mistakes. Undoubtedly, you'll relate to their situations and have a chance to think of what your response will be for the real challenges in life.

Each week is broken down into five devotions. You can do one a day during the week. You can do them on weekends and take off the busy days in the middle of the week. It is flexible.

Let it fit your schedule. At the end are questions to make you think, including some that are great to share with a group. So you and your friends can go through the devotions together if you want. Or you can make it part of your small group.

The first week is all about leading by example. The choices you make influence others whether you think of yourself as a leader or not. The five *C*s of leadership can help you become a leader with character! You'll be challenged to think of *C*reative, *C*ompassionate solutions to alleviate other people's needs. You'll see that *C*haracter and *C*ompetence go hand-in-hand with effective leadership. And you'll be challenged to find the *C*ourage to reach out to your circle of influence.

Take a week to read real stories from real people and make your own decisions about living the Christian life as an example. At the end of each day is a simple statement to help you "own" your choices. Check the box when you feel you are ready to claim that choice. If you aren't sure, keep on digging to bring the truth of God's Word into your heart and the courage of leadership into your life.

ichoose to creatively Help others

Antonio was the kind of guy nobody bothered. His teachers dreaded finding his name on their class rosters each semester. Like coming face-to-face with a pit bull, underclassmen never made eye contact with him. Antonio was a trouble-maker, drug dealer, and bully…until the life-changing night he spent in jail.

Antonio cried in his jail cell most of the night. In desperation, he called out to God to save his life from the mess he created. He didn't know much about God, but when he prayed he believed God would hear him. Antonio's choice began a new chapter in his life. In the days and weeks that followed, he learned what it means to be a follower of Jesus and he dedicated himself to the journey.

Back to school

When Antonio went back to school after this life-changing experience in juvenile jail, he was a man on a mission to help others in his high school come to know God personally. Ostracized from his old group because he no longer did drugs, Antonio searched out other outcast students and invited them to sit with him at lunch. Sitting next to Antonio meant you weren't picked on. In his mind, Antonio called it the "safe table."

The safe table gave Antonio an opportunity to impact students at his school. Through the relationships he built, he was able to share his faith and see many others come to a saving faith in Jesus too. Antonio had eternal impact at his high school. At the end of the year, the teachers selected Antonio for the Student Most Changed award.

creativity counts

If impact is the mark of leadership, creativity is one of the means to achieve it. Antonio was a creative leader who initiated incredible change in the lives of his peers. He saw where he could help others at his school and developed the strategy of the safe table. It isn't what others may have done, but it worked.

Jenna and Betsy's creativity helped feed thousands of kids all summer long. When the two young ladies heard that little kids from low-income families miss meals when school is out of session, they developed a creative solution they called "Block Out Hunger."

With the help of a few dozen friends, they hung brown grocery bags on door knobs in neighborhoods all over town. Each bag had a note stapled to it that invited the homeowner to fill the bag with food and leave it on their front steps the following Saturday.

Block Out Hunger collected over 80,000 cans and boxes of non-perishable food for local food shelters at the time of the year when donations were needed most. Jenna's and Betsy's creative solution was a success because it was so simple—for the participants *and* the organizers. Passing out bags door-to-door took less time than it takes the mailman to walk down a street. Creativity counts!

Find Your creative Flair

God gives each one of us unique personalities, talents, and gifts. So why is there such a demand to be the same as everyone else? What can you do to tap into your unique creativity to impact your world for God? College students across the country are unleashing their creative solutions to meet real problems:

- Greg feeds 200 homeless men every Tuesday night with his dollar campaign to buy McDonald's double cheeseburgers.
- Lisa organizes garage sales to raise money to buy life-saving medications for an orphanage in Haiti.
- Kaitlyn uses Facebook to encourage her friends to join her in mission work in Vietnam.
- Marilyn makes donations to help build a church in the Congo in the name of friends and family—in lieu of buying birthday presents.

- Daniel leads "Man Time," a guys accountability group and Bible study, on his freshman dorm floor.
- Jessica runs a day camp out of her house and teaches Bible lessons to kids in her neighborhood each summer.
- Robbie invites many guys—his entire baseball team—to his college ministry overnights; they send a private bus to pick the team up.
- Amy invites non-Christian friends to church each Sunday and takes them out to lunch afterward.

Just like Josh and the safe table, we all have opportunities to promote change and impact others for Christ. Matthew 5:16 instructs us to let our "light shine before men." As we use our unique gifts and find creative ways to let God's light beam through us, God will be praised. Shine on!

iThink

1. Describe a creative solution to a need or a problem that you have seen. _____

_____

_____

2. What does creativity have to do with leadership? _____

_____

_____

_____

3. What are some of the obstacles that keep us from thinking creatively about promoting change? _____

_____

_____

_____

4. Share an idea of how to impact others for Christ. _____

_____

_____

_____

 Check here if you choose to find creative ways to help others.

THE NERD

ichoose compassion

Everyone thought Kyle was a big nerd. Carrying a big stack of books home on a Friday afternoon, he was like a walking bulls-eye for the bullies who picked on him. They ran at him, knocked him to the ground, and laughed as his books and wire-rimmed glasses flew in the air. With tears in his eyes, Kyle sat humiliated on the front lawn of the school. That's where he met Brad.

Brad was a confident, compassionate guy. Athletic and smart, he was well-liked. He helped Kyle back on his feet and offered to carry some of his heavy load of books. As they walked home, the two guys discovered they lived just a block apart. Brad invited Kyle to play football with his friends that afternoon, and the two eventually became best friends.

Fast forward to senior year. Kyle, the class valedictorian, was the graduation speaker. The one-time nerd was now one of the best looking, most popular guys in school. In his graduation speech, he testified to the power of his friend's compassion. Brad was shocked at what Kyle said.

He talked about the day he met Brad; it was the same day he was planning to kill himself. Kyle was carrying all his books home so that his mom would not need to clean out his locker after his suicide. Kyle was lonely and at the end of his rope. Brad's simple act of compassion—a helping hand, a genuine interest—not only initiated a great friendship, it saved Kyle's life.

The Good Samaritan

Jesus told the story of the Good Samaritan to teach us about compassion:

> A Jewish man was traveling on a trip from Jerusalem to Jericho, and he was attacked by bandits. They stripped him of his clothes, beat him up, and left him half dead beside the road. By chance a priest came along. But when he saw the man lying there, he crossed to the other side of the road and passed him by. A Temple assistant walked over and looked at him lying there, but he also passed by on the other side. Then a despised Samaritan came along, and when he saw the man, he felt compassion for him. Going over to him, the Samaritan soothed his wounds...and bandaged them. Then he put the man on his own donkey and took him to an inn, where he took care of him. The next day he handed the innkeeper two silver coins, telling him, "Take care of this man. If his bill runs higher than this, I'll pay you the next time I'm here." (Luke 10:30–35, NLT)

The story of the Good Samaritan is impressive not just because he helped the Jewish man, but because, out of everyone who walked by, he was the least likely to help.

Samaritans and Jews just flat out did not like each other. The irony is that if the roles would have been reversed, the Jewish man probably would not have stopped to help the Samaritan.

as ourselves

Compassion is deep awareness of the suffering of someone else coupled with the wish to relieve it. Just like the story of the Good Samaritan, Brad couldn't walk by Kyle when he was knocked to the ground. Compassion welled up within him as he saw someone suffer and he was moved to do something about it. Brad set an example of compassionate leadership without really thinking about it.

It almost sounds cliché, but the simple truth from God's Word is that we are to love others as ourselves. Think for a second what a big idea that is—*as ourselves*! It seems like most of us are looking out for number one first and worrying about others second.

What is your natural response to seeing others suffer? To help find out, finish the following thoughts:

- When the entire class is disrespectful to the teacher, I....
- When my good friend needs a shoulder to cry on, I....
- When I see someone without a friend, I....
- When I think about my standard of living compared to the homeless and deprived, I....
- When I think about the eternal destination of my friends who don't know God, I....

In the case of Kyle and Brad, Brad treated Kyle as he would have liked to be treated in the same situation. Brad didn't know it at the time, but his reaction saved Kyle's life. Being a Good Samaritan can be life-changing.

iThink

1. What are the roadblocks to loving others as ourselves—especially those who seem unlovable? _____

_____

_____

2. Share a time when you treated someone in a tough situation as you would have liked to be treated. _____

_____

_____

_____

_____

3. Describe an example of when someone has done the same for you. _____

_____

_____

_____

_____

4. On a scale of one to ten, how compassionate are you? Where would you like to be on the scale, and what's one idea of how to get there? _____

_____

_____

_____

_____

_____

● Check here if you choose to lead with compassion.

NOBODY'S LOOKING

ichoose to do the right thing

Jen filled her gas tank to the brim and sped away before anyone could notice the problem. You might have done exactly the same if you were in her shoes. Technically, she didn't do anything wrong. Technically.

After a long shift waiting tables at a pizza place, Jen had stopped for gas and a soda on her way home. Before she began fueling, she noticed a problem with the meter. Other customers noticed it too. In fact, many of them were making calls to their friends, telling them to race down to take advantage of the situation.

Earlier that night, the gas station attendant accidentally typed the decimal in the wrong place when he set the price of gas. What was supposed to cost $2.10 was selling for only $0.21—just pennies on the dollar! Realizing what was happening, Jen decided to pay at the pump and skip going inside to buy soda.

Jen's adrenaline rush from scoring cheap gas quickly turned to feelings of guilt as she drove home. She had a check in her conscience—confirmation she had exploited the honest mistake of the gas station employee. Jen turned her car around and drove back to pay for her gas and let the attendant know of his mistake before the station lost thousands of dollars.

True character is revealed when nobody's looking. It is built by doing the right thing in those tough situations. In Jen's case, nobody in the store knew about the mistake with the gas pricing. It was totally up to her whether she would be a person of uncompromising character or just another person taking advantage. In the excitement of the moment, she failed. But ultimately she made an honorable choice.

When It's Not So Easy

We're faced with hundreds of chances each day to flex our good character muscles. When life is good, it's easy to make the right choices. When times are tough, however, character is truly tested. People model strong character by the choices they make every day:

- A young man protects his girlfriend's purity and keeps his own physical desires in check by setting physical boundaries for their relationship.
- A young woman keeps her promise to her parents to never drink and drive.
- Overwhelmed by finals, a college student considers cheating, but decides to study through the night instead.
- An employee is tempted to call in sick to go Christmas shopping, but works her shift and goes shopping on her own time.
- A stranger finds a lost wallet and returns it to its owner.

- A teen-ager wakes up every morning twenty minutes early to pray and read the Bible.

Your character is who you are. The stronger it is, the more equipped you are to live for God and experience life abundantly. When we think of character like a muscle, we can see each trial in life as the resistance that will help our muscles grow strong.

A character-defining moment

Two college friends couldn't have been more different when it came to academic strengths. One was phenomenal at math but terrible in English; the other was an English wiz but couldn't do math to save her life!

The girls were similar in height and hair color, so early in the semester they decided to switch places for a test in their respective weakest subjects. The plan seemed foolproof. The English major reasoned that she'd never really use trigonometry in real life anyway—it seemed like a waste to bother studying. The math major was just as apathetic about brushing up on her English skills. They each just wanted to pass their classes and never look back.

In the days leading up to the switch, each girl had second thoughts. They weren't afraid of being caught even though it could lead to being expelled from the university. It was a matter of conscience. Cheating on the tests was just wrong and they knew it. In the end, each girl took her own exam (and passed!). Faced with a difficult decision, the girls flexed their strong character muscles and came out stronger on the other side.

pure in Heart

Matthew 5:8 says the pure in heart will see God. The pure in heart go beyond doing what's easy, convenient, or profitable. They do what's right no matter what. When it comes to character, there is a lot at stake.

How well will you do the next time nobody's looking? Don't be fooled—there is no such time! God sees every situation, knows our every thought, and says character counts. He will bless us when we make decisions that honor Him during those tough moments.

i think

1. How would you have reacted in Jen's situation at the gas station? Why? _____
_____
_____

2. What was at stake when the two college girls planned to swap tests and cheat together? _____
_____
_____

3. When you think about an area of character in your life that you'd like to strengthen, what comes to mind first? _____
_____
_____

4. How you react to the moments in life that go wrong reveals true character. What does this mean? _____
_____
_____

● Check here if you choose to do the right thing when nobody's looking.

BARNABAS NOTES

ichoose to step out in courage

High school guys typically aren't into note writing, especially to other guys. Some would even call that weird. But when Adam returns to his small Christian high school each year he brings notes for every guy in his class. Nobody seems to think it's weird.

At the beginning of the school year, Adam writes a personal message to each guy in his class. The idea would work for any small group like a soccer or volleyball team, youth group, or choir. Adam fills each note with encouraging words specific to each guy—words like:

- "Thank you for setting such a great example to all of us by being so kind. I've never heard you say a negative word about anyone."
- "I admire your heart for God. When you pray before lunch, I am encouraged to be bold in my faith too."
- "You are the funniest person I know. Studying with you makes homework fun!"
- "I don't know you very well, but I am thankful you're on our team. Nobody gives more effort at practice than you. Way to go!"
- "You rock—how can one person be so gifted? You have more musical talent in your pinky finger than I have in my entire body!"
- "I know you're dealing with tough stuff at home. Psalm 119:7 is for you today!"

At the end of each note, instead of signing his name, Adam signs "Barnabas." That's the name of one of the most encouraging men in the Bible. The name actually means "encourager." Adam's "Barnabas notes" mean so much to some of the guys, they keep the notes taped to their bedroom mirrors or save them in dresser drawers for years.

It's no wonder the guys like Adam's notes. What's not to like? The notes make them feel good. Adam is a gifted communicator and a thoughtful friend. Even more, Adam is courageous. He chose to act knowing he risked being laughed at or labeled "weird." But he did it anyway. Sometimes leading by example means standing up where others would not.

courageous leadership

Being a leader often means acting alone and hoping others follow your lead. Leaders don't let the pack control their actions, they makes choices according to their convictions. Adam exhibits leadership by writing Barnabas notes to other guys. He isn't concerned about how many other guys write notes. He doesn't spend time worrying about how he'll look. He steps out in front, ahead of the pack, and courageously encourages others.

I learned a lot about being a leader one of the first times I went to a movie with a girl alone. It was a big deal too, because she was old enough to drive and I wasn't. After a great pizza, our next stop was the movie theater. That's when the night took a turn for the worse.

The movie we picked was supposed to be a light-hearted comedy. It turned out to be sexually-charged and inappropriate. I was uncomfortable—I would have never knowingly taken a girl to see that movie. But I froze in my seat. What if she liked the movie? I didn't want her to think I was a little kid for wanting to leave. After all, it was only rated PG-13. A few more minutes into the movie, Sara stood up, looked down at me, and with disappointment on her face and in her voice she said, "I don't know what you're going to do, but I'm leaving." And she walked out.

Ugghh! I knew I had blown it. I had a chance to be the leader in the relationship, but I lacked courage to take the first step. Sara was forced to action. I've never forgotten what it felt like in that moment of failure. Ever since, I've been determined never to experience those feelings again by being too timid to do what I know is right. Thanks to Sara, I learned a big lesson about courageous leadership that day.

God often commanded leaders to be strong and courageous (see Joshua 1:9). Sometimes being courageous means stepping out before anyone else steps out. Sometimes it means speaking when nobody else speaks or refraining when others fail to refrain. Courageous leaders inspire, serve, and enrich the lives of those around them by being the first one to stand up for what is right.

ithink

1. Name a way to serve or encourage others that might require courage. _____

_____

_____

2. Describe a time when it was difficult for you to stand firm in your faith. Did you lack courage or exhibit courage? ____

_____

_____

_____

_____

3. What advice would you give to someone who spends too much time worrying about what other people think? _____

_____

_____

_____

_____

4. Finish this thought: a person who lacks courage to stand firm likely lacks.... _____

_____

_____

_____

_____

_____

_____

_____

_____

_____

_____

_____

Check here if you choose to step out with courage.

RESERVED

ichoose Thoughtful Leadership

Seniors know they're a big deal. Having climbed the social totem pole for years, they are ready to take their rightful position as top dogs on campus. They may even feel entitled to it after years of paying dues and watching other seniors bask in glory.

Senior year, however, is also filled with lots of "lasts." The last homecoming game, the last school dance, and the last school retreat. And thank goodness there's the last set of final exams. Maybe that's part of the reason being a senior is such a big deal—the clock is ticking and time is slipping away. After high school, seniors separate and move away to all parts of the country to begin their life experiences at the bottom of the totem pole. After college, seniors move way in search of job opportunities where they are again at the bottom of the totem pole.

The Last Retreat

The seniors at Southwest Christian High School were in charge of planning and hosting the all-school spring retreat. Determined to make the most of their last retreat, they put a lot of work into the details ahead of time. When the day of the retreat finally came, the seniors arrived before everyone else to make sure their plan worked like clockwork.

The school had four school buses and one luxury coach bus. The coach bus was fully equipped with air conditioning, TVs to watch movies, reclining seats, and a bathroom. As a first order of business, they reserved seats before the underclassmen arrived.

When the freshmen, sophomores, and juniors showed up, the seniors were ready to welcome them. Each younger student was treated like royalty. The seniors blew whistles, waved pom-poms, and made a big fuss over each one. They ran out to the cars and carried their sleeping bags and duffle bags. Every underclassman received a care package filled with treats, keepsakes, and notes of encouragement from every senior.

When it was finally time to board, everyone approached the buses to find the luxury coach bus already reserved. There was a big sign draped across the outside of the bus that read: "Reserved for our awesome freshmen!" The seniors took their seats on a dumpy old school bus for their last-ever high school retreat. Their selfless attitude and careful planning made a big impression on everyone else that day. In turn, they had more fun than they had ever had before. Perhaps the best indication of the seniors' influence came in the years to follow. Their legacy of thoughtful leadership was continued by those who had once followed.

Leaders set the tone

Dr. Martin Luther King Jr. was the youngest person in the world to receive the Nobel Peace Prize when it was awarded to him in 1964. He is remembered as a great American leader although he never held an elected office. Dr. King set the tone for millions of Americans—young and old, black and white—for non-violent protest against segregation in the United States. So great was his influence in the Civil Rights movement, he has his own national holiday.

Mrs. Covington is an inner-city high school teacher. At her school, less than 45 percent of the students graduate, much less go on to college. The computer lab is empty because the school district is nearly broke. Gang violence is growing, fights occur daily, and students are out of control. Except in Mrs. Covington's class. At five foot two, Mrs. Covington is not an imposing figure. She does not yell, she does not push. But she sets the tone in her class by carefully treating all students with the decency they crave. She demands respect by the way she gives respect. Her classroom is like a calm island in a sea of raging waters.

Where do you have opportunities to be a careful leader? What circles do you run in where a few years in age or unique life experiences put you in a position of natural leadership? Do you:

- have a little brother or sister?
- help train new people at work?
- play sports on a team with new recruits?
- excel in a certain area of study where others struggle?
- attend a youth group or college group with younger students?

There is someone looking up to you whether you realize it or not. Watch carefully for opportunities to influence. Just as the seniors at Southwest learned, careful leadership means looking for opportunities in places we don't always think to look. It sets the tone for things to come.

iThink

1. Name a time when you felt entitled to the perks of being one of the older ones in a group. _____

_____

_____

2. How does leading by example inspire people to follow? __

_____

_____

3. What's one way to help set the tone for future leadership in your circle of friends? _____

_____

_____

4. Name three benefits of being thoughtful when reaching out to others. _____

_____

_____

_____

_____

_____

● Check here if you choose to be a thoughtful leader.

DEVOTIONS

WEEK TWO

FOR REAL LIFE

the relationships I choose to keep

Do you know the president of the United States? You could probably identify him by face or voice. You may even know a thing or two about his political platform, religious beliefs, family life, or hobbies.

In the 1980s most people knew that President Reagan's favorite treat was jelly beans. In the 1990s everyone knew

President Clinton enjoyed Big Macs. In recent years, the entire country watched to see what kind of dog President Obama would pick to live in the White House with his two young daughters. Americans know a lot about their presidents. But to *know about* the president is different than to *know* the president.

Authentic relationships are the result of intentional effort, time, and investment on a personal level. They're a *two-way* street. Authentic relationships are the opposite of phony and superficial time-wasters. Authentic relationships add richness to life.

Contemplate your relationships with friends and family. When others see you coming, do they see a dump truck backing up with lights flashing and warning beeps blaring? Or do they see the Energizer Bunny who takes a licking and keeps on ticking?

How about your relationships with the opposite sex? You're faced with choices every day that will either help build authentic relationships or will contribute to destroying those same relationships.

Authentic relationships are a choice. So are worthless ones. You get to choose which you will nurture and which you will avoid. Which will you choose?

ATM$

ichoose to invest in friendship

Spencer lived in a house with six other guys. (You can almost smell the dirty socks and mystery meat in the fridge just thinking about that!) Spencer's roommates became his best friends. For two years, they shared food, clothes, computers, and friends. They had a blast sharing life together in close quarters. To Spencer, it felt like they shared everything but chores. He always got stuck washing dishes, vacuuming, and taking out the garbage because nobody else would. He was beginning to resent his friends, and bitterness was creeping into his heart.

In the fall, the giant oak trees blanketed the yard with leaves. One day, Spencer was visibly upset as he raked by himself. His five buddies sat inside watching sports on TV. Spencer never asked for help. He thought his friends should have noticed he was doing all the work and offered to help. Fat chance.

Spencer is extremely considerate. He's the kind of guy who would look out the window, see a friend working in the yard, and immediately run out to help. So when his friends didn't respond the same way, he felt taken advantage of.

Have you ever experienced being let down by a friend who didn't seem to contribute as much to the relationship? How about the flip side of that—have you ever been the friend who benefited from the other's investment, but did not contribute back? Spencer was investing a lot in unbalanced relationships. To keep bitterness from growing in relationships, it is important to make sure friendships are equally invested.

Going Bankrupt

Jenny made all the effort in her relationship with Alicia. She initiated every phone call, every visit, and every contact. Jenny gave thoughtful gifts to Alicia on her birthday and at Christmas. And for four years, all through college, she treated Alicia to lunch once a week. Jenny deposited. Alicia withdrew and withdrew. Eventually, Jenny felt unappreciated and severed the relationship. When Alicia broke up with her boyfriend and needed a good friend to lean on, Jenny was long gone.

Relationships are like bank ATMs—they only work when there are both deposits and withdrawals. Customers who only withdraw money eventually run out. And friends who only take from a friendship and never deposit eventually bankrupt the relationship.

What to do?

Each person is unique and invests in friendships differently. Which of the examples below represent your efforts to invest in relationships?

Circle the ones that you connect with the most:
- Speaking or writing words of encouragement.
- Pursuing spending time together.
- Taking initiative to call or keep in touch.
- Being more interested than interesting.
- Showing consideration by being helpful or willing to serve.
- Showing friendly affection like hugs, and pats on the back.
- Being quick to share.
- Giving thoughtful gifts.
- Other: _____

To have healthy relationships, it is important to strive for a good combination of withdrawals and deposits. While you can't control what someone else will do, you can certainly choose how to invest and protect yourself.

Be aware of the friend who only withdraws. Your relationships deserve investors—and recipients. You are worth investing in! And when others do invest in you, you'll have more to give away!

Need ideas for investing in your relationships? Try a few of these, but don't be afraid to add your own ideas:

- Send a note.
- Go out of your way to thank or help someone.
- Buy a friend a coffee or soda.
- Call someone you haven't called for a while.

Try many different things. Make sure your ATM accounts have plenty of deposits.

iThink

1. Have you ever had a friend who seemed to withdraw and never deposit. How did that impact your relationship? _____

_____

_____

_____

_____

_____

_____

2. Name one person who does a great job investing in you?
What does this friend do? _____

_____

_____

_____

3. Identify one relationship where you are lacking in
deposits. How can you deposit into that person this week?

_____

_____

_____

_____

4. When might it be the right time to walk away from a
relationship? What do we need to consider before doing so?

_____

_____

_____

_____

_____

_____

Check here if you choose to invest in balanced
relationships.

COOL BEFORE US

ichoose to honor my parents

Before we were born, our parents were probably cool. They had more money and they spent it on themselves. Their cars had fewer doors. They went out at night and came home late. They were thinner and in shape. Then we came along. Kids are expensive and a lot of work. We changed their lives. Our parents' cool factor today is a product of many years with us!

Isn't it ironic that most of us go through a stage where our parents embarrass us? It's usually sometime around junior high or high school when our parents suddenly become humiliation machines, especially in public. It's like *we* forget that for years we were the ones who threw up on *their* friends and threw temper tantrums in public. After all that, how do we have the nerve to be embarrassed by them?

It's normal to see tension between children and parents. But starting in your teens and twenties, it's important to start building a great foundation for a grown-up relationship with your parents. Deuteronomy 5:16 reminds us of God's command to "honor your father and mother…so that it will go well with you." Honoring our parents is a critical step in our continuing development from child to adulthood. Without intentional effort, it's easy to grow up in every other area of life and miss growing up in the way we relate to our parents. What makes it so critical is that honoring parents is ultimately choosing to honor God.

Like wet cement, the goal is to set the foundation as you want it before it settles and hardens. Here's a quick inventory for you to evaluate how your foundation for a grown-up relationship with your parents is shaping up:

- Do you talk to your parents like you talk to other adults you respect?
- Do you ever initiate spending time with your parents?
- Are you more responsible at home than you were a year ago?
- Do you say "I love you" to your parents?
- Do you play by the house rules?
- Do you ask your parents for advice?
- Do you want to have a closer relationship with your parents?
- When you mess up, do you apologize to your parents?
- Do you pray for your mom and dad?

How did you do? Are you satisfied with your relationship with your parents? It is up to you to create a positive, growing friendship with them as you get older. Brittany and Jon came up with brilliant ideas.

Brittany's story

Multiple sclerosis won't kill Brittany's mom, but it will leave her in a wheel chair in the prime of her life. As her immune system attacks her brain and spinal cord, she will slowly lose control of her body over a period of many years. For Brittany, it's painful to think about the day when her active mom, so full of life today, will be held hostage by a ravaging disease. Her mom walks five miles every evening so she can remain in peak shape and fight off the MS as long as she can, but signs of deterioration are showing. Brittany can see her mom beginning to physically slip away.

Her last summer at home before leaving for college, Brittany worked like a maniac. Most days, she babysat from early in the morning until late in the afternoon. In the evenings she cleaned homes in her neighborhood. Brittany worked and saved all summer so she could buy her mom a therapeutic bed for her birthday. The love her mother felt that day probably soothed the aches in her body for months to come!

valuable gift

A college recruiter met with Jon for pizza to talk about playing soccer and potential scholarships. Over the course of small talk, Jon revealed the ups and downs he had experienced with his parents during high school. He was constantly at odds with his mom and dad. But the summer before Jon's junior year, he made a life-changing decision to start living for Christ.

Later, Jon's mom told the recruiter more about the changes in her son. For her last birthday, he wrote her a note on plain notebook paper. "I promise to give you a hug and say 'I love you' every day until I leave for college." The recruiter asked the mom if her son was making good on his promise. She smiled with pride and said, "He hasn't missed a day." The words Jon wrote were more valuable to her than anything he could have purchased. The recruiter was so impressed with Jon's maturity and care for his mom he gave Jon a scholarship!

Honor

Brittany and Jon both gave their moms amazing gifts. One was very expensive and the other didn't cost a penny. Their motive behind the gifts was a genuine desire to *honor* their mothers.

The idea of honoring moms and dads isn't anything new. In fact, God places such a high value on honoring parents, He included it in the Ten Commandments. Out of everything important to God, honoring moms and dads is in the top ten!

1. On a scale of one to ten, rate your attitude and actions toward your parents. _____

_____

_____

4. Describe a time when it was difficult to honor your parents. _____

_____

_____

2. What could you do daily to honor your parents in attitude and action? (Honor curfew, helping around the house, etc.)

_____

_____

_____

3. What's one big thing (like Jon's promise) you could do to show your parents honor? _____

_____

_____

_____

Check here if you choose to honor you parents.

LIFELINES

ichoose to select friends wisely

When John Carpenter won the grand prize on ABC's popular game show *Who Wants to be a Millionaire*, he used his phone-a-friend lifeline to answer the final question. Before John ever played the game, he gave careful consideration to who he would call in case he needed help making a big-money decision.

We'd all do the same thing. Before going on national television to play for a million dollars, we would think long and hard about who to call as a critical lifeline. Most of us will never appear on a TV game show, but we all choose friends in real life. The friends we choose impact the quality of our lives.

Who would you pick for the following roles? Think outside of your limited friend group to include anyone your age.

• If you had a twin sister, which guy your age would you trust to date her: _____

• If you could choose one peer to be your boss for your entire career, who would you choose: _____

_____

• If you were in a coma and had to trust someone to make an important decision for you, who would you pick to make that decision for you: _____

_____

However unlikely these three scenarios are, each answer reveals a lot about what you think of the people you selected... and even more about the people you didn't pick.

All Three

So whom did you pick in each scenario? After considering character, respect, and fairness, did you pick your best friend to date your sister? After contemplating work ethic, wisdom, and discernment did you pick the last person you hung out with this week to be your boss? After considering wisdom and discernment, did you pick anyone in your close circle of friends to make the major decision for you? Your answers tell you a lot about *what you really think* of your friends. Your answers reveal if you think your friends are worth keeping.

Brandon is the friend I'd pick for all three situations. I think so highly of him, I've actually asked him to date my sister (I told him I'd pay for the wedding!). For a while, I also thought I'd end up working for Brandon—he is so sharp and hardworking I knew he'd be successful. And on several occasions, although I wasn't in a coma, Brandon has guided me through important decisions. He even selected my last car. I've learned that I have been blessed with a friend who is trustworthy, fair, and wise.

quality versus quantity

Janie worked hard to be popular—and popular she was. Getting ready for school was as big a production as the Academy Awards. Hair! Make-up! Wardrobe! If getting ready for school was like backstage at the Awards, walking the halls was like the red carpet. It was all about being seen with the right people.

Like a scene out of the movie *Mean Girls*, Janie built herself up by tearing others down. She was always making up rumors and spreading gossip, even about her friends. One day, she really outdid herself. She made a list of critical things about almost every girl in her grade and shared it with a friend.

You guessed it—the list went public. By lunchtime the campus was abuzz and Janie was too ashamed to show her face. In her quest to make herself look better to one friend, she alienated herself from everyone. Deep down, Janie didn't even like her friends very much. And after the list spread, her friends realized it.

Alyssa's experience was different. In high school, her group
of friends became big time potheads. For years, Alyssa was
too. But when she decided to give up that lifestyle, she lost her
former friends. Suddenly they wouldn't give her the time of day.
Although it was painful at first, Alyssa realized that real friends
would have celebrated her turn from drugs.

Janie and Alyssa both could have used a friend or two with the
qualities that inspire trust. The book of Proverbs says "He who
walks with the wise grows wise, but a companion of fools suffers
harm" (13:20). One good friend is more valuable than a posse of
fools. That's why it is so important to choose them carefully.

iThink

1. What surprised you about the names you picked to fill in
the blanks in this chapter? _____

_____

_____

_____

2. What was the toughest part about trying to think of a friend you'd trust or follow? _____

_____

_____

_____

_____

3. Why would or why wouldn't you show up on your friends' list of trustworthy friends? _____

_____

_____

_____

_____

4. In your experience, have you seen any examples of Proverbs 13:20? _____

_____

_____

_____

_____

_____

● Check here if you choose to be choosy about your friends.

NOT YET

ichoose marriage before sex

Ashley's mom had "the talk" with her when she was sixteen. Fighting back tears of fear, her mom explained the importance of birth control. She sent a mixed message. On one hand, she expected Ashley to remain a virgin until marriage— she definitely did not approve of sex outside of marriage. On the other hand, she wanted Ashley to know how to use birth control in case she would decide to live by different standards. Ashley's mom thought the worst-case scenario would result in an unplanned pregnancy. But is that really the worst-case?

Ashley's mom may have missed the biggest danger of all when she had "the talk" with her daughter. Each one of us has sexual purity to protect—purity that affects our relationships with others, our relationship with God, and the way we see ourselves.

Sex outside of marriage can bring consequences even greater than babies or catching diseases. Sex affects us not only on a physical level, but on an emotional and spiritual level too.

It would be bad news for Ashley's mom to have a pregnant daughter. But even worse would be a sexually active daughter who jumps from boy to boy, and man to man throughout her teens and twenties, leaving a part of herself with each of them—having been tricked into believing she was "protecting" herself from pain and consequence.

An Amazing Invention

Sex is amazing. After all, God invented sex. According to the Bible, sex is the thing married couples do. Wait a second. What do you call it when unmarried people have sex? Isn't that the same thing?

The answer depends on if you agree with God—the Creator of sex—about what sex really is. In the Bible, there are three different words used to describe what we think of as sex. In God's eyes, only one situation equals "sex":

Between:	The Bible calls it:
a married man and woman	sex
an unmarried couple	fornication
a married person and anyone other than the spouse	adultery

God made the act of sex for a husband and a wife to experience together—period. It's so sacred He won't even call it sex when the same act is mimicked outside of marriage. My grandma used to refer to her scissors as the pizza cutter because she used it to cut pizza. But the rest of us know that pizza cutters and scissors are different, so we use different words to describe the two. What matters is that we know the difference.

We need to remember what sex really is when we talk about having great sex. It's only possible to have great sex in marriage—everything else is a cheap knockoff. And everything else brings painful consequences.

you can bet on it

Taking something as awesome as sex and warping it into something other than God intends *doesn't* work. It's a recipe for pain—you can bet on it.

Adultery and fornication:

- damage your relationship with God
- damage or kill your relationship with your partner
- destroy the trust in your relationship with your spouse

stuck

Try gluing two pieces of tissue together and let the glue dry. It would be impossible to pull the tissues apart without ripping them. Once delicate materials like tissues are bonded, separation gets messy. When two bodies bond through a sexual relationship or experience, part of each person always stays with the other. It's a biblical truth—Mark 10:8 says, "the two will become one flesh. So they are no longer two, but one."

Remember, God's design for sex is marriage. We're meant to bond like superglue with one person and stay bonded. This is the best way to experience the most committed, trusting, and intimate human relationship possible. For people who aren't married, the answer isn't "no" to sex—the answer is "not yet."

What are your physical boundaries and limits? As you decide how far you will go, consider:
- The more time you spend alone, the more intimacy increases.
- The further you go, the more difficult it is to go back.
- It's not about how far you can go, but how much you can save.

iThink

1. Why do you think God has different words for sex in the Bible? _____

_____

_____

_____

2. How can sex outside of marriage bring consequences even more painful than an unplanned pregnancy or STD?

_____

_____

_____

3. "A fire in the fireplace is a good thing, but fire on a carpet can quickly get out of control." What does this statement have to do with setting sexual boundaries? _____

_____

_____

_____

4. If you were to draw a line on a piece of paper and mark each progression toward sex (hug, hold hands, cuddle, kiss, French kiss, make out), where would you set your boundary or limit? _____

_____

_____

_____

_____

_____

⬤ Check here if you choose to save sex for marriage only.

WEEK2//DAY5
DOOR DINGS

As early as girls begin thinking about their weddings, boys begin dreaming about muscle cars and big trucks. At eight years old, each is infatuated and delusional at the same time.

Sean's dream car became his real car on the morning of his 18th birthday. On his way out of the house, he found a brand new red Corvette convertible in his driveway—a gift from his grandpa. This car had everything he wanted: special rims, a sweet sound system, and a high performance engine that would take him from zero to sixty mph in four seconds. This car was not only incredibly cool, it was incredibly expensive.

Sean's perfect car received its first blemish in the Target parking lot later that day. He came back from shopping to find a door ding. With less than ten miles on the odometer, Sean's car was already showing signs of wear and tear. He was devastated.

Put yourself in Sean's shoes—what would be his best reaction after discovering a door ding on his brand new dream car? Should he:

- beat dents into his car with a sledge hammer?
- slash the tires and break in the windows?
- douse his car in gasoline and set it ablaze?
- abandon his car and start riding the bus?

Sean did not resort to any of the extreme measures listed above. Instead, he learned a lesson about being more careful. He decided from that day forward to park in the back of parking lots, far from other cars. He wanted to try his best to avoid any more door dings. Even with the ding, his car was still tremendously valuable, and he wanted to preserve as much of its value for as long as possible.

But I've already gone too far

Just like Sean's expensive car, sexual purity is valuable and worth protecting. It's easy to feel like there's no going back after crossing sexual boundaries. It often feels like purity is so fragile that one door ding is the same as a torched car.

Kevin made a commitment to himself to wait until he was married to have sex. One night in college, he became drunk at a party and had sex with a girl he barely knew. The next day, he was sick to his stomach knowing that he sacrificed something so special and important on a one-night stand.

Katie always wanted to wait until marriage to have sex. She believed it was worth waiting for because it forms such a physical bond. She only wanted to form that kind of a bond with one man—her husband. Like Kevin, Katie made a mistake. But unlike Kevin, she was not drunk. Her sexual regret stemmed from a slow slide of compromising boundaries with her boyfriend. Kissing turned into touching, sitting turned into lying down, and making out turned into sex over a period of months. Then they broke up. Katie, who once felt strongly about physically bonding with only one man, began having sex with every guy she dated. She felt like her purity was flushed down the toilet, so it didn't really matter anymore.

Most of us have made mistakes that we wish we could take back. It's especially difficult to deal with that regret when it involves sexual mistakes. But our bodies are kind of like the Corvette—full of value and worth preserving, even after a ding or a dent. It's never a wise choice to become so disappointed in yourself that you treat your body like a pile of junk.

two choices

So what do you do if you've already gone too far? What if you regret crossing physical boundaries or becoming sexually active outside of marriage? You can make a decision today to agree with God about how valuable you are and try harder to protect your purity.

A special word to Girls

Girls, there truly are guys out there who are committed to their purity and who will be committed to yours too. You are so valuable and precious—you deserve to find a guy who believes the same about you and treats you with respect. Pray that God will open your heart to the guy who is right for you.

A special word to Guys

Every girl dreams of being swept off her feet. She is waiting for you! Don't buy into the lie that says the more women you sleep with, the more of a man you are. A real man has self-control. A real man strives to protect her purity as well as his own. Pray that God will open your heart to the girl who is right for you.

If you feel like you've already gone too far, don't be fooled by the Devil into believing your purity is gone and your body is a piece of junk. You are still highly valuable, worth protecting and preserving.

1. Have you ever lost or damaged something of great value?
How did you react? _____

_____

_____

2. Do you think of your sexual purity as something prized
and valuable? _____

_____

_____

3. Why is it easy to think once a sexual boundary has been
crossed, it doesn't matter how many more times it's crossed?

_____

_____

4. Are you ready to set new sexual limits today? _____

_____

_____

_____

_____

_____

 Check here if you choose to protect your purity.

DEVOTIONS

WEEK THREE

FOR REAL LIFE

The Lies I choose to overcome

Lies are bad.

Would you want to make a big decision based on information
full of lies? What if you were going to buy an expensive
new television but the salesperson failed to mention it was
defective. In the box it looked new and shiny, but once you
opened the box you found two things: a TV that didn't work
and the no-return policy. You'd feel duped.

Would you want to fly on an airplane that was piloted by someone who wasn't trained to fly a plane? What if he lied at the gate and somehow made his way to the cockpit but he wasn't really a pilot after all? (That's actually happened before!) His lies would put your life in jeopardy.

You probably fall for lies all the time. We all do. We want to trust people.

Satan is the Father of Lies. That means he's always lying and he's pretty good at it. In fact, there is no better liar around! His goal is to lie, cheat, and steal to keep you from following God. He knows exactly where you'll fall for his lies, so that's usually the route he takes. If he can get you to believe even a few of his lies, he can hurt you deeply. And nothing would make him happier than to hurt you and keep hurting you.

This week we'll examine five lies straight from hell—and we'll debunk the lies with truth straight from the Word of God. These are lies many people buy into. Lies like:

- Everyone is having sex...so why shouldn't I?

- I'll change when I'm older...but I'm having fun now.

- I can't overcome my problems...so why even try?

- The Christian life is boring...it's not for me.

- The good outweighs the bad...that's all that matters.

Wouldn't you like to make your big decisions based on truth, not lies? All it takes is a simple two-step process. Step one is to identify what the lies are. Step two is to make the right choices based on that identification. As you read through the chapters, think about which of these lies you fall for the easiest. By letting God's truth guide you, choosing truth over lies gets easier and easier.

EVERYONE'S DOING IT

ichoose to do what's right

Steve came to college as a freshman ready for a new beginning. Just months earlier, he came to faith in Jesus and started living his life for God. A new school, new set of friends, and new environment was the fresh start he needed. Steve was determined to be a young man of God and a leader on his campus.

As the leaves changed colors and autumn arrived, Steve found himself with a girlfriend. Her beauty and charm caused him to fall head over heels for her. They had so much fun on their first date, they went out the very next night. But by the end of the second date, Steve's heart was already filled with regret.

Back in high school, Steve believed that as long as he wasn't having sex, everything else was fine. But this time he didn't feel the same way. After the second date, they were already involved physically and he felt guilty.

Steve reached a crisis of decision. He was faced with ignoring his guilt or making a change. He decided that he wanted to treat her differently—better—than any guy had ever treated her. He wanted to respect her body and protect her purity. He wanted to be the leader in their relationship (versus going as far as she would *let* him go). Steve asked for forgiveness and asked for a fresh start. Moving forward, they decided to hold hands and hug—that's it.

How many guys do you know like Steve? Guys who have enough humility to apologize for being selfish, guys with enough sensitivity to consider how girls feel deep inside?

How many guys do you know who care more about protecting their girlfriends than about what they can get from their girlfriends? Word got around on campus about Steve, and other girls started looking for guys like Steve. He is an inspiration to all of us to live by a higher standard, to honor God with our bodies and guard our hearts from sexual sin.

what are the facts?

Let's separate fact from feeling. For most of us who aren't having sex, it feels like everyone else is having sex. But is that so?

Before answering that question, consider another: does it matter? After all, most people are in credit card debt. Does that mean you want to be in credit card debt so you can fit in? Most Americans are overweight. Does that mean you wish you could be overweight too? Divorce is pretty prevalent these days. Does that mean you dream of getting divorced? It's not always ideal to follow what it seems everyone else is doing.

But in reply to that first question, the answer is a loud and clear "NO. Everyone is not having sex." Among high school students in ninth through twelfth grade, less than 50 percent of them have experienced sex. That means *more than half* are not sexually active. Usually the ones who are having sex talk about it much more than the ones who aren't, so it feels like more people are doing it. Even beyond high school and college, there are millions of young men and women waiting until marriage to have sex. Some are even famous for it:

• Tim Tebow is an outstanding football player for the Florida Gators. During his years in college, he was as well known for his commitment to wait until marriage for sex as he was for being the first sophomore in history to win the Heisman Trophy.

• NBA champion A. C. Green played for the Lakers and other professional teams for fifteen years. Sometimes he gained more media attention for being a virgin than he did for winning games. By the end of his long basketball career, Green not only set a record for playing more consecutive games than any other player in NBA history, he also retired from the sport a virgin (and married a wonderful woman who was grateful he waited!).

The fact is not "everyone" is having sex. Many young men and women are choosing to wait for marriage. They are rejecting compromises like making out in secret or justifications like "oral sex isn't 'real' sex." Ephesians 5:3 says to not allow even a hint of sex outside of marriage. That is pretty straightforward. Just wait. No compromises. No justifications. God wants you to be pure for Him and for your future spouse.

iThink

1. Why are guys like Steve in such short supply? _____

_____

_____

_____

_____

_____

2. If 55 percent of the vote is considered a landslide victory in politics, why do we believe 55 percent of teens not having sex is a minority? _____

_____

_____

_____

3. What kind of pressure do you think Tim Tebow and A. C. Green put up with? How do you deal with some of the same pressures? _____

_____

_____

_____

4. What compromises or justifications about sex are widely accepted today? How do you think that has changed in your generation? _____

_____

_____

_____

_____

 Check here if you choose not to do what everyone else is doing.

ichoose self-control NOW

"I'll change when I'm older, but I'm having fun now," Mariah said. Sweet and fun, Mariah was also self-destructive. She could drink with the best of them, although the rest was a blur. She was a notch on many guys' bedposts. She was popular and bright, but going nowhere fast. Mariah fell for the lie that being young is a great excuse for being wild. In her mind, there would be plenty of years in the future to settle down.

The Devil would love for us to believe that the way we live our lives doesn't matter. But the truth is, sin disguised as "fun" is really just a trap, and it gets us every time.

When all of Mariah's friends started to marry, she found herself lonely and regretful. Where was her good man? Why wasn't God helping her? One courageous friend warned Mariah about being too quick to blame God. After all, she may have missed a good man or two along the way when she was spending her time with the wrong kind of guys. Mariah was faced with the painful realization that she fell for sin disguised as fun.

A Good Name

It takes a lifetime to build trust and only a moment to lose it. Brian lost a great deal of his parents' trust when he lied about staying at a friend's house. Brian had really driven out of town for a weekend at a cabin. Nothing "bad" was going on at the cabin, but he knew his parents would not allow him to go unchaperoned. The fun Brian had for two days was not worth the disappointment he felt for breaking his parents trust. He was determined to restore his good name with the people he loved most: his mom and dad.

How does one go about restoring their good name? By committing their way to God's way (Psalm 37:5). That calls for consistent faithfulness, and time. In the beginning it was frustrating for Brian to sense hesitation or doubt from his parents, even as he worked so hard to be trustworthy. But time simply had to do its part, and Brian had to be patient, committed to God's way.

Being trustworthy is important for every young person because it follows us into adulthood. Carrie attended a private Christian college with rules about community life. Every student was required to sign a covenant agreeing to abstain from alcohol while living on campus. Carrie signed the covenant with no intention of honoring it. She rationalized her drinking by telling friends it wasn't a problem for her because she never got drunk. She was of legal age and she drank responsibly, so the covenant was stupid, she said. Plus, she was having fun. Carrie's problem didn't have to do with alcohol; it had to do with her word. Since her word didn't mean much to her, it didn't mean much to other people either. If she wasn't a woman of her word on a small issue like this, would she keep her word for something really important? The Bible says, "Whoever can be trusted with very little can also be trusted with much, and whoever is dishonest with very little will also be dishonest with much" (Luke 16:10).

There's no such thing as just having fun now, and changing when we get older. We are who we are. If we embrace dishonesty, sex, drugs, drinking, excess eating, pornography, and other harmful traits today, those traits begin to harden like cement as we age. Researchers say our dominate traits are easy to mold and shape in our teens, but begin to harden in our early twenties. "I'll change later," isn't as easy as it seems.

Trained to crave

Justin looks at porn in his dorm room most nights before bed. It's easy because he has a single dorm room. Justin's justifications for watching porn sound an awful lot like "I'll change when I'm older, but I'm having fun now."

What Justin doesn't realize is that he's training his body and mind to crave impurity. Each time he feeds his mind porn, he's

Justin is open and honest about his porn habit because he doesn't think it's a problem. He rationalizes:

- As a young man, his hormones are raging.
- Better to look at porn than actually have sex.
- It's no secret; all of the guys he knows look at porn too.
- It's natural to be interested in girls.
- His sin is no worse than anyone else's sin.

feeding that impurity. It affects the way he views women, the way he views himself, and it affects his relationship with God. Justin thinks porn won't be an issue once he gets married because he'll be having sex with his wife. But after years of filling up on impurity, the purity of sex with his wife won't fulfill his cravings. He will still crave porn.

Just like Mariah, Brian, Carrie, and Justin, we are faced with temptation to believe lies from the Devil that tell us it doesn't matter what we do. We wish we could have fun today and make a change tomorrow. But the truth is we are robbing our future with our "fun" today.

iThink

1. Have you damaged a relationship by living for the moment and planning to change later? Explain. _____

_____

_____

2. Why do you think it is easy to put God on hold with big promises to "do better when we get older"? _____

_____

_____

3. Describe a situation when you had to work to rebuild trust over time. _____

_____

_____

4. Can you come up with a plan of action to change an area of your life that you have been making excuses for? _____

_____

_____

_____

● Check here if you choose to change now—not later.

ichoose not to let "can't" win

Jake hasn't laughed in years. In fact, he has barely smiled. One night, he hung his head in shame and shared a journal entry with his support group. In the entry, he wrote about how he got mad during his parents' painful divorce and took his frustrations out on his younger sister by hitting her. He wrote about a homosexual relationship in which he was involved with one of his close friends. Jake had someone else read the words he could not say about the shame he carried.

Some of us experience a great deal of hardship in life, while others not as much. Adversity, however, hits all of us eventually. The hardships below represent a variety of levels of adversity. Can you relate to any of them?

- A poor black girl born in rural Mississippi was shipped between family members most of her childhood. Beginning at age nine, she was molested and raped by a family friend, a cousin, and an uncle. At fourteen, she gave birth, only to see her premature baby die within weeks.
- A wiry high school sophomore tried out for the varsity basketball team but was rejected for being too short.
- A teenage boy dropped out of high school, moved into a YMCA, and worked full-time at a fast food restaurant.
- A businessman went bankrupt and lost his cars, homes, and all of his money.

Tragic stories, right? These people would have been justified in saying, "I can't." Instead, they became some of the most well-known characters in popular culture. You might be familiar with them:

• The poor black girl who was raped is Oprah Winfrey. Today she's the most popular TV talk show host and first black female billionaire in the world. She's a friend to presidents and movie stars alike. She's talked about the pain in her life on her show and helped countless Americans find the courage to tackle their own pain.

• The wiry basketball player is Michael Jordan, one of the greatest professional basketball players in history. He grew four inches the next year and went on to win two Olympic gold medals, six NBA Championships, fourteen NBA All-Star awards, various special recognitions and all-time records. Not making the team as a sophomore motivated Jordan to work extra hard that year and come back stronger and better.

• The high school dropout who went to work at a fast food restaurant was Dave Thomas. Dave went on to create the Wendy's franchise. At the time of his death, there were over 6,000 Wendy's restaurants because of his good ideas about fresh food and fast service. Dave made a point to earn his high school diploma forty-five years after he dropped out. His graduating class that year voted him most likely to succeed!

• The bankrupt businessman is Donald Trump. Instead of living in the streets, Donald got his act together and created one of the best known development groups in the United States. His name adorns huge skyscrapers all across New York and other cities. These days, people and celebrities even compete on television to become his apprentice!

It's a destructive lie to say that it's impossible to overcome obstacles and pain. The point is not to emulate all of their values or philosophies, but there's no argument that these four famous people demonstrated determination and refused to let nasty circumstances define their lives. It would have been so easy to wallow in the miserable conditions they found themselves in, but instead they looked at what they could become.

Laugh Again

The book of Philippians says, "He who began a good work in you will carry it on to completion" (1:6). This is a verse to cling to in times of frustration and failure. It's a note from God to His children to remind us that there is no circumstance or problem too big for God. He started something in you and He will give you the strength to see it through to the end—even if you fail a lot before you get there.

Remember the story at the beginning of this chapter about Jake? He made a decision in his support group to not be defined by the problems of his past. He's working hard at moving on. He's growing in his personal relationship with Jesus and experiencing God's all-encompassing forgiveness. He's even begun to laugh again.

Forgiveness and confidence from the Lord transforms lives. Recently, Jake turned his attention from the adversity in his life to sharing his life with other people. As he began to say to himself, "I can," he began to see himself as a valuable child of God.

iThink

1. What struggles seem to knock you and your peers down the most? _____

_____

_____

_____

2. What does it mean to not let your circumstance define your life? _____

_____

_____

_____

_____

3. How do the stories of Oprah Winfrey, Michael Jordan, Dave Thomas, and Donald Trump encourage you to look at the pain you've encountered? _____

_____

_____

_____

_____

4. Do you need to make a decision to overcome something painful in your life today? What is it? Do you believe God cares enough to help you through it? _____

_____

_____

_____

_____

_____

●   Check here if you choose to believe "I can."

B.O.R.I.N.G.

ichoose to have fun within boundaries

When it comes to basketball, I need every possible advantage. My friends who like to play basketball don't like to play with me. Why? Because I make up my own rules. I count every basket I make as three points—no matter where I shoot from. I shoot from out-of-bounds or in some cases at the wrong basket, and count all baskets I make. I give myself do-overs when I miss. The saddest part is that even with all of my antics and cheating, I still can't seem to win a game.

Playing by my rules is fun for me, but not so much fun for others. It is frustrating to play a sport with someone who doesn't respect the rules. When we all have the same rules, we know what to expect and how to play together. Rules make sports fair and fun.

Most people think boundaries and rules suck the fun out of life. They think the Christian life is boring. But living God's way is just the opposite of boring. It's the best life possible!

Isn't the christian life boring?

Charlie loved Twinkies, Skittles, bubble gum, and Mountain Dew. As much as he loved sweets, he hated brushing his teeth. So he stopped when he was eight years old. Every time his mom told him to brush his teeth, he closed the bathroom door and ran water for a minute to fool her. But the next time Charlie went to the dentist, he had eight cavities—so many, the dentist couldn't fix them all at once. Charlie had to return two more times for drillings and fillings. In retrospect, Charlie regrets not following his mom's instructions.

God's Word is our instruction book for life. He loves us so much that He gives us boundaries and rules to protect us. When we do what He says, good things will happen later on. When we go against God, bad things will happen later on. It's that simple.

You might wonder if the Christian life is boring. With a Bible full of "rules," is all the fun drained out of life? Charlie thought his mom's rule about brushing his teeth was boring, so he didn't do it. But the consequence was many more trips to the dentist to painfully fix the holes in his teeth. Likewise, God's guidelines are meant to keep us from painful consequences and give us the best life possible. When we follow God, we never sacrifice anything good.

Great Sacrifice/Great Reward

To achieve the best life has to offer requires sacrifice, wouldn't you agree? What sacrifices must be in place to achieve awesome results like:

- buying your first car?

- becoming an all-state athlete?

- graduating from college?

- winning an Olympic gold medal?

- owning your own home?

- getting married?

- having kids of your own?

- retiring with financial security one day?

If you've ever saved money for something like a car, you know it takes hard work and sacrifice. Saving requires saying no to lots of other purchases. But the reward is your very own car!

in step

Conditioning and disciplining ourselves as Christ-followers enables us to live life at peak performance. The more in step you are with God, the better life will be. Instead of boring, the Christian life is rich.

For those who are faithfully pursuing the Lord, the Christian life brings:

- peace of mind
- great joy
- comfort in times of challenge and sadness
- freedom from the bondage of sin
- forgiveness and saving grace
- direction in life that produces confidence

Next time you hear people say the Christian life is boring, you'll know the truth. The Christian life brings the best in life through God at work in you.

ithink

1. Give examples of the best rule and the worst rule ever imposed on you. _____

_____

_____

_____

_____

2. What's one boundary or guideline you're grateful for
(speed limits, traffic signals, laws about guns, etc.)? ———

_____

_____

_____

_____

3. What kinds of sacrifices are required to live in a way that
pleases God? ———

_____

_____

_____

_____

4. How it is helpful to compare the sacrifice and rewards
of living for God to the sacrifice and rewards of winning an
Olympic gold medal? ———

_____

_____

_____

_____

_____

● Check here if you choose to have fun within
boundaries.

GOOD PEOPLE

Some people say that grandchildren are parents' rewards for not killing their kids.

Marilyn loved spending time with her grandchildren. She fed her grandkids sugary treats that they'd never get at home. When eating out, the kids could order anything they wanted because "Grandma's paying." As the kids became teenagers, their friendship with Marilyn deepened. They went camping together, out to movies, and talked every few days on the phone. Marilyn was an incredible grandma—I know because Marilyn was *my* grandma.

Years later, a call from the hospital came early in the morning. Grandma wasn't doing well. Pneumonia was attacking her old body beyond her strength to fight it off. The doctors encouraged us to visit with her while she was still alert, before she slipped away.

As I drove to see her that day, I prayed and asked friends to pray for me. "Lord, I'm going to share my faith in You with Grandma. Please give me the strength to talk with her without becoming emotional." Although Grandma would do anything to please her grandkids, I wanted her to make a decision to accept Him into her life—but not for me. I wanted her to genuinely turn to Jesus before she died.

As Long as the Good outweighs the Bad, Right?

For her entire life, Marilyn was uncertain about God. Like many of us, she hoped she did enough good in her life to qualify for heaven. And good she was. She shared everything she had, even when she had next to nothing. She donated to food shelves and loved to feed anyone who was hungry. She didn't judge people. Grandma hoped she was good enough for God, but she couldn't be sure she was.

That day in the hospital, I talked about sharing. I told her that all of my memories of her were of her sharing—her food, her time, her words, her hugs. Then I told her the best thing I could share with her was my faith in Jesus Christ. She could know God personally. She said she was ready.

The Romans Road

The Bible is clear about our need for a personal Savior. It's just as clear that accepting Jesus Christ as our Savior is the only way to be saved from our corrupt human nature. The Book of Romans presents a clear roadmap to faith in Christ with five simple verses. These verses changed Marilyn's life. Her final days on earth were spent in peace knowing her Creator. Her eternal destiny was changed once and for all because she chose to believe that:

1. Everyone needs a personal Savior.

   "For all have sinned and fall short of the glory of God."

   (Romans 3:23)

2. The consequence of sin is death.

   "For the wages of sin is death, but the gift of God is
   eternal life through Christ Jesus our Lord." (Romans 6:23)

3. Jesus Christ died to cover our sins.

   "God showed his great love for us by sending Christ to
   die for us while we were still sinners." (Romans 5:8 NLT)

4. We receive salvation and eternal life through faith in
   Jesus Christ.

   "If you confess with your mouth, 'Jesus is Lord,' and
   believe in your heart that God raised him from the dead,
   you will be saved." (Romans 10:9)

5. Salvation through Jesus Christ brings us into a
   relationship of peace with God.

   "Therefore, since we have been made right in God's
   sight by faith, we have peace with God because
   of what Jesus Christ our Lord has done for us."

   (Romans 5:1 NASB)

Coming to faith in Jesus is the only way to know God personally and to experience forgiveness for the sin that keeps us from God. Jesus is our only way to eternal life in heaven. Being saved from hell (eternal separation from God) has nothing to do with the good outweighing the bad.

Real Faith

Faith in Jesus begins with God initiating a relationship with us by drawing our attention to Him. Have you ever felt a tug on your heart to accept Jesus as your Savior? Maybe you already have. If not, are you ready to invite Jesus to come into your life, and are you ready to follow Him?

To receive Jesus in your life, pray a simple prayer to God. There are no magic words. Just express your genuine desire to have Jesus come into your life, save you and forgive you, and be in control of your life. After that, just believe.

iThink

1. Who is the "best" person you know? What makes them good? _____

_____

_____

2. What's the problem with thinking that heaven is sure "as long as the good outweighs the bad"? _____

_____

_____

3. Describe how you came into a personal relationship with Christ, or why you're not ready to yet. _____

_____

_____

4. Have you ever shared the message of Jesus' salvation with someone? What would help you better share Jesus with those around you? _____

_____

_____

    Check here if you choose to trust in Jesus.

DEVOTIONS

WEEK FOUR

FOR REAL LIFE

The Life I choose to Live

Have you ever said to yourself, "I believe in God, so now what?"

Making the decision to follow God is the first choice in a lifetime of choices as a Christian. Yes, it's a choice to believe. But it's also a choice to live every day like you believe. The toughest part of the Christian life is that it's so daily. You have to wake up and choose God every day.

Can you imagine getting married to your college sweetheart, and never seeing that person again? Once the wedding ceremony ended, going your separate ways? Would you say to yourself, "Now that the ceremony is out of the way, I can go back to my old life"? Of course not—that would be ridiculous.

But that's what so many Christians do. They make a big decision to trust in Jesus. And after the thrill of the moment goes away, so does their commitment to Him.

The Bible does not call us to merely believe. After all, even the Devil himself believes in Jesus. We are called to become Christ-followers. We're called to follow our Savior, make Him the Lord of our lives, and make our lives count for Him.

In the same way that marriage vows are just the beginning of marriage, asking Jesus into your life is just the beginning of a lifelong relationship with Him. It's just the beginning of a lifelong process of choosing to follow Jesus each day.

This final week is filled with stories of real young people who have decided to live for Christ. What's true for them is true for you too—nobody can make the decision for you to follow Him. It's your choice. Making that kind of commitment affects everything from big decisions like selecting a college to daily words we choose to speak. Where are you in your relationship with the Lord? Do you choose to live for Christ?

BE PREPARED

What would you guess are the top vacation destinations during spring break? At the top of your list might be the white sand beaches of Florida, the warm temperatures of Hawaii, or the sunshine of Mexico—all great places to vacation.

There is a place that has more sand than the other places combined, has hot summerlike temperatures, and has sunshine almost every day of the year. It's a place we're all familiar with, but it's not too big on tourism. Where is that, you ask? Iraq!

Battle zones are real and dangerous and we're glad they're far away. But there is a big battle zone that every young person will face when he or she leaves home. It's not a geographical battle zone, but it is just as dangerous. It is a spiritual battle zone.

agent of change

You may not think of college as being a battle zone, but it is. Choosing your battleground is very important. When it comes to choosing a college, there are many factors to consider. It's one of the biggest expenses in life—second only to buying a house. It is the training ground that, in many ways, determines the trajectory of a person's future. It's the place many young people meet their spouses. And choosing a college is often the *first* big decision a young adult makes. With so much at stake, how do you choose?

Location, cost, programs offered, scholarships, housing, sports, and friends also attending are important considerations. But choosing a college strictly on these factors is as naive as choosing spring break in Iraq for the sun and sand. In both cases, we need to acknowledge the dangers.

scary odds

More than seventy-five percent of Christians who live for the Lord in high school walk away from their faith in college. Those are scary odds! The reason? We walk onto a battleground not even realizing there's a battle. We should only enter into battle when we are aware it's going on and only if we're dedicated to winning.

David's parents wanted him to go to a Christian college, but David ultimately picked a non-religious, private college for the battleground of lost people. David had a passion to impact the football team for Christ. He knew he'd have a greater opportunity to impact people for God at a school full of unbelievers than at a Christian college. David went to college like a missionary going to work. Over his four-year college career, David impacted countless students with the message of hope in Jesus, an opportunity he might not have had at a Christian college. While he was there he earned a degree and played football too, but those were his secondary priorities.

David is a great example of someone acting as an agent of change. But beware—unless a person is determined to go to a battlefield as an agent of change for God, it's more likely that he or she will be changed by that place.

what if i'm strong?

Picture the strongest guy you know—someone with raw, brute strength. If he were to stand on top of a five-foot stool, and you were to stand on the ground, would it be easier for him to pull you up or easier for you to knock him down? You would sooner knock him off the stool than he would pull you up. The strong are not invincible when they're in a vulnerable position. Unfortunately, spiritual strength and rootedness in the church doesn't make us invincible on a spiritual battleground.

Jodi was a strong Christian, a leader in her youth group. But by the end of her sophomore year in college, her values had slowly been corrupted to the point that she was distant from God and doubting her faith. Instead of having an impact on others, Jodi was impacted and changed. Her relationship with God was the weakest it had ever been at the time she was making the biggest decisions of her life: whom to date/marry, which career path to choose, where to live. She ended up making decisions she would never have dreamed of making.

what's best for you?

David's example of storming a secular campus for Christ is an exception. His first priority was to reach others for Christ, and this led him to where he could have the biggest impact possible. Jodi had different priories and ended up choosing a place she wasn't ready for. She couldn't possibly stand strong when the spiritual battle wasn't even on her radar.

A Christian college can be a good choice unless God is calling you to make a difference as a shining light in a dark place. These years could prove to be integral in developing warriors ready for a lifetime of spiritual battle. You can make a commitment, like David did in college, to be an agent of change throughout your life—not just in college, but also in the workplace and in the world around you.

Be careful to base your choices on what is best for your spiritual life as well as your intellectual life. You don't want to end up in Iraq when you are expecting Daytona Beach.

ithink

1. How is a college campus like a battlefield when it comes to the Christian walk? _____

_____

_____

2. What was/will be your first concern when selecting a college? _____

_____

_____

3. Do you think of college as more of a battle zone, mission field, or a training ground? _____

_____

_____

4. What other examples of big decisions will give you the opportunity to be an agent of change or be changed? _____

_____

_____

_____

_____

⬤ Check here if you choose to be prepared for spiritual battle.

ISSUES OF THE HEART

ichoose to watch what I say

Douglas was the meanest kid in school. He had a special knack for knowing exactly how to rip someone apart with his words. He routinely made his teachers cry, and he humiliated scores of classmates on a daily basis. Douglas was cruel. Douglas was a broken young man on the inside.

One morning, after being verbally assaulted by Douglas, a guidance counselor replied to him, "Hurt people hurt people. For you to say such ugly things to me makes me feel sorry

for you. You must have a lot of hurt built up inside of you."
Douglas's eyes filled with tears—he had been discovered.
Deep inside, Douglas was a miserable human being. And the
worst part of all was that someone else knew.

The words that come out of our mouths reveal much more
than we realize. Our mouths are like windows that open right
into our hearts. The book of Matthew says that it's "out of the
overflow of the heart the mouth speaks" (12:34). To a large
extent, we have control over what we say. But there comes a
point when our true hearts are revealed and we speak what we
know. If there's a problem with our speech, it's more an issue
of the heart than an issue of the mouth.

Clearly, Douglas's words were hurtful to others and hurtful to
God. He was outright mean. But "outright mean" words aren't
the only words that we should be concerned with.

Lackadaisical Banter

Two buddies and I went to Boston for a long weekend. For
four days, we ate amazing Italian food in the North End of

town, bummed around Harvard Square, relaxed in the Boston Commons, and caught a Red Sox game at historic Fenway Park. The three of us are big jokers, so we constantly teased each other—all in good fun. But by the second day of our trip, we realized that we were missing a great opportunity to build each other up with our words. We weren't saying anything truly bad, but we weren't saying much good either. We were so careless with our words, constantly joking and shooting sarcastic darts at each other, we failed to say much of anything that was actually helpful or beneficial.

My friends are awesome—as soon as we acknowledged the opportunity, we all made great efforts to improve. We looked to Ephesians 4:29 as a blueprint for our speech. Our next few days together were drastically different. We shared some of the best moments we've ever shared together, rich in conversation and authentically encouraging. The lackadaisical banter was replaced with genuine talk, and it changed each of us.

This is what our blueprint for speech looked like:

"Do not let any *unwholesome* talk come out of your mouths, but only what is *helpful* for building others up according to their needs, so that it may *benefit* those who listen" (Ephesians 4:29, emphasis mine).

How awesome is that? The verse not only says what *not* to do, it's says what *to do* It's easy to tell if our speech is on par with God's perfect standard. Just ask yourself three questions:

1. Are my words wholesome or unwholesome?
Wholesome means good and decent. Speech turns unwholesome when we corrupt it with gossip, lies, slander, swearing or foul language, sexual joking, or words of hate.
2. Are my words helpful?
Helpful words are easy to spot because they encourage, edify, teach, correct (in love), praise, tell the truth, comfort, and bring humor.
3. Are my words beneficial?
Jim told a funny story at the dinner table about a sports

injury that could have left him unable to have children. While the story would have been well received by his friends, his younger sisters were uncomfortable with the subject matter. Jim wasn't being crass or dirty in telling his story, but he didn't think through some important guidelines to determine if it was beneficial to everyone in the room. To know if speech is beneficial, ask these questions:

- Is this appropriate to share in this setting?
- Is this appropriate to share with the opposite sex?
- Is this the best timing to share my message?
- Does this add value to others in any way?

Since your words are a window into your heart, what do you want others to know about you and your God when they look through that window? (You may need to clean a little dirt off the window. But it will be worth it.)

iThink

1. If your words are a window into your heart, what do you think others see? _____

_____

_____

_____

2. What does "hurt people hurt people" mean? _____

_____

_____

_____

3. Which part of the "blueprint for our speech" do you excel in (wholesome, helpful, beneficial)? _____

_____

_____

4. Which part of the blueprint do you struggle with the most (wholesome, helpful, beneficial)? _____

_____

_____

_____

● Check here if you choose to only use words that are wholesome, helpful, or beneficial.

AUDIENCE OF ONE

ichoose to focus on god, not others

Jill is one of my smartest friends. She has an amazing ability to inspire those around her and motivate change. She's a natural leader and a gifted communicator. And her personality is strong and outgoing. When Jill is in the room, everyone knows it.

In the course of starting a new ministry, Jill received constructive criticism from a well-meaning friend. She was warned about coming on too strong and being too aggressive. After all, people can be timid around fast-talking movers and shakers. Jill adapted her style the next week and took a softer approach with her team. The softer approach sparked new feedback from another friend. He warned Jill to be more assertive and direct with people. For a few weeks, it seemed everyone had an opinion on who they thought Jill should be.

Jill was discouraged and on the verge of burnout. She shared with me that one person gave this advice and another said that, and then she asked me what I thought she should do. My answer (gained from experience): just be Jill.

Jill's problem wasn't that she was too aggressive or too timid. Her problem was that she became so focused on trying to please everyone else that she lost where her focus should have been: pleasing God.

audience of one

Have you ever been so busy trying to please everyone else that you forget to try to please God? We can definitely learn from others how to improve ourselves, but we can't live our lives trying to be who everyone else wants us to be.

God wants us to be who He made us to be. In Jill's case, He made her to be a strong leader. Much of what she'll learn along the way will come from coaches and mentors. But Jill will need to be true to who God has called her to be. We serve an audience of One—God Himself. At the end of the day, He is the only One we need to please.

Four Distracters

Outright sin is a clear way to keep from pleasing God. But there are other distractions in our lives that are mainly good, like parents and friends. The bottom line is this: no distraction from God is acceptable. Four of the most common include:

1. Trying to Please Friends

Madalyn's friends told her she talked too much, so Madalyn stopped talking. She held her thoughts inside and bit her tongue. She beat herself up for being "annoying." That would have worked, except it left Madalyn miserable. She is a bubbly, outgoing, entertaining person. Eventually Madalyn figured out a way to move past her insecurity—she started talking again. And if her friends didn't like it, they really weren't her friends at all. Real friends love each other for who they are.

2. Trying to Please Coaches/Teachers/Bosses

When Greg stopped playing football after his freshman year of college, the coach who recruited him was disappointed—and he let Greg know it! He told Greg he was selfish and had let the team down. Greg faced tremendous pressure not only from his coach, but from parents and teammates too. You know what Greg's reason was for not playing football? He had a vision to feed homeless men in the inner city. Greg was true to his calling and developed a program that year to feed hundreds of men every week. All because his focus was on pleasing God before anyone else.

3. Trying to Please Parents

After her junior year in college, Nicole was inspired to take a six-week mission trip to India. But her father couldn't understand the logic of missing the opportunity to work and earn money for school. For eighteen years, she was taught that honoring meant obeying. Now as an adult, she felt like obeying her dad would mean disobeying God. Nicole went to India, but took careful steps to make sure her dad felt heard and valued. She went out of her way to treat him with respect while explaining her choice to please God. Eventually, he came around. Nicole's mission trip not only gave her the opportunity to minister in India, it gave her a chance to minister to her own father as she followed God wholeheartedly.

4. Trying to Please Ourselves

Mike dreamed of finishing college and landing a job that paid big money. Somewhere along his journey through school, he stopped asking God for direction. Mike eventually found his dream job with a big paycheck. The problem was, he formed his dreams without including God…and God's dreams are always bigger and better than ours. His dream job ended up being a nightmare and carried him further from God.

Don't fall into the people-pleasing trap that so easily takes our focus off of God and away from His best for us. The Bible tells us to keep our eyes on the prize—and the prize is pleasing Jesus.

iThink

1. How have you tried to change yourself to please someone else? _____
_____
_____

2. Of the four distracters, which one can you relate to the most right now? _____
_____
_____

3. Name a specific way you've experienced each distracter. Give specific examples of people and experiences. _____
_____
_____

4. How do you please God instead of people? (Think of your answer and then read the next chapter!) _____
_____
_____
_____

○ Check here if you choose to live your life for an audience of One.

GET IN THE GAME

ichoose to start playing

Mandy, Brianna, and Carley have a lot in common. They were seniors in high school the same year and captains of their volleyball teams. Brianna and Carley were ranked in the top ten players of the state. Mandy was good enough to play on the varsity team as a freshman in college. These girls were so good at volleyball, they were each offered scholarships to play at Division I universities. The biggest coincidence is, all three girls chose to attend a small Division III college.

Their decisions had to do with their love of the game. Even with so much talent, they knew that they would spend the first year or two warming the bench at a Division I school. But at a smaller college with a smaller program, they'd get court time all four years. And that's what they wanted the most—to get in the game.

more than drills

What if you trained hard, did everything necessary to excel in your favorite sport and be the best, and never got to play? As a serious athlete, you did it all—two-a-day practices, drills, extra practice, conditioning, sprints. But what if that was all there was—just training? What if you never actually got to play the game? After a while, you'd probably get bored and lose interest. You'd think to yourself, "This isn't worth it—the time commitment, the training, and the diet." You might even walk away from the sport all together.

There is an interesting parallel between sports training and our Christian faith. Think of your Christian community and all that comes with it as your practice and conditioning for a sport.

However, instead of two-a-days and conditioning, we have:

- youth groups, camps, and retreats—amazing experiences that can nurture our faith in God and development as Christians.
- Bible studies to help unlock the power of God's Word.
- mentors and leaders to invest in us, much the way coaches invest in athletes.
- sermons and classes to root us in God's truth for daily living.

Youth group and Bible studies are tremendous activities to be involved in, but Christians ought to think of these activities as conditioning or practice. The real game—loving God, loving others, and sharing our faith—isn't inside the walls of church or at youth group. It's out in the real world.

Why do you think seventy-five percent of Christians who live for God in high school walk away from their faith by the time they finish college? A big part may be because they never get in the game. Their faith is crowded out. They spend years conditioning and practicing at church and with Christian friends, but eventually they're bored, lose interest, or decide it isn't worth the perceived sacrifice to live for God anymore.

Are You in the Game?

Andy was washing his face before bed in the dorm bathroom when James bumped into him. James knew Andy had had a date that night with a girl he met at church. He asked Andy if the girl was spending the night with him. What could have been locker-room bragging became a faith-sharing experience. Andy told James that he had a great date and that he walked her home safely before returning to the dorm. When James didn't understand why Andy didn't try to sleep with her, Andy talked about his faith in God. Right there in the dorm bathroom at two in the morning, James prayed to receive Jesus. Andy's personal faith story was just what James needed to hear— Jesus was what he had been searching for.

Do you think that conversation encouraged Andy in his faith too? You bet it did! He was so excited he woke up a few of his Christian friends to tell them about what had happened. Andy got in the game and boldly shared his faith, and the payoff was huge. He helped change the eternal destination of a good friend! Philemon 1:6 tells us to be active in sharing our faith with unbelievers so we will "have a full understanding of every good thing we have in Christ." In other words, when we don't share our faith, we're missing out on a big part of knowing Jesus.

24-Hour challenge

In the next day or so, do you think you can get in the game and share your faith with someone else? Christians have something very special to share. For the person who has not come to receive Christ, life is full of uncertainty. In these days of social networking, it's easier than ever to strike up a conversation with everyone from a best friend to a long-lost friend. A word from you on your own faith journey, even if you don't have all the answers, might impact someone else in a life-changing way. Try it. You can make a difference.

iThink

1. What types of things do you do to build up your faith?

_____

_____

_____

_____

2. Describe a time when you lost Interest in living out your Christian faith. Were you sharing your faith at that time?

_____

_____

_____

_____

3. What's your biggest roadblock in talking about your faith with friends? _____

_____

_____

_____

_____

4. Who is one person you think would benefit from hearing your faith story? _____

_____

_____

_____

_____

_____

_____

● Check here if you choose to get in the game and share your faith.

GOD WANTS YOU

ichoose to give god myself

Today, more kids than ever like vegetables. Not the kind we eat—but the kind that sing! Bob the Tomato and Larry the Cucumber are familiar names to most of us who grew up watching Veggie Tales cartoons. The Veggie Tales series of videos, shows, and movies are the most successful faith-based cartoons in history.

Phil Vischer, creator of Veggie Tales, lost his multi-million dollar media empire almost as quickly as he built it. Today, he speaks to groups across the country about the years he spent dreaming up a big idea for God, and the painful process of losing his company. Phil had been so busy coming up with ideas of what he could do for God he forgot about maintaining his relationship with God. In the end, he realized all God ever wanted was Phil the person...not what Phil could do. Losing his company was a blessing in disguise, because Phil made the main thing the main thing again—he invested in his relationship with God. Some of us may make a big splash for God with an idea like Veggie Tales, and some of us may make lots of little ripples for Him. It doesn't matter—God wants *us* whether we bring ripples or floods—as long as we are obedient to Him.

God cares More about Direction than Perfection

Once we get the idea of being perfect Christians out of our minds and replace it with the idea of being Christ-followers, we'll be in good shape. What does it mean to follow Christ? It means to put Him at the center of our lives instead of isolated in a single God-compartment in our lives.

In his own home, my garbage man might be a dad who dotes on his children or a loving husband who provides for his wife. He may be the star slugger on a local softball team or one of the regulars at a neighborhood restaurant. To his friends, he might be a reliable confidant or a poker buddy. To me, he's just the garbage man. It's easy to divide our lives into small pieces in order to fill the different roles expected of us. But God only wants us to fill one role—that of a Christ-follower.

In the example of the garbage man, here's what that would look like: He'd be a *Christ-following* man who collects trash. At home he'd be a *Christ-following* dad who dotes on his children or a *Christ-following* husband who provides for his wife. He may be the *Christ-following* star slugger on a local softball team or a *Christ-following* regular at a neighborhood restaurant. To his friends, he might be a *Christ-following* confidant or a *Christ-following* poker buddy. Being a Christ follower is a full-time job.

Many presidents of the United States have said that the hardest part of the job is always being president. There are no days off. Everything they say is officially on record. They represent 300 million Americans with every step and every word. Even on vacation, the president has a military aide at his side with the codes to unleash nuclear weapons. Since the president is the only one who can authorize such force, he carries that burden of responsibility with him to every event, from his children's birthday parties to family vacations. Being president may be the closet thing we can compare to the type of dedication following Christ requires. There are no pause buttons or vacation days from that following Christ—you're either following Him or you're not. You have to choose.

Fully Devoted

Let's say you were babysitting a five-year-old boy and he did something so naughty you sent him to his room. But after sending him to his room, you see that he stopped halfway there. Instead of going all the way to his room, he went as far as the stairs and sat there. Would you be pleased? No! Going part way and stopping short is outright defiance.

Christians stop short of following Jesus all the time. Semi-pure or mostly-good intentions are really just bad intentions in disguise. First Corinthians 10:31 says, "Whatever you do, do it all for the glory of God." The word "whatever" covers everything. Here are ten simple things you can do to start living for the glory of God:

1. Excel in sports for the glory of God.

2. Forgive someone else for the glory of God.

3. Share something of yours for the glory of God.

4. Break a bad habit for the glory of God.

5. Start a good habit for the glory of God.

6. Speak kindly for the glory of God.

7. Learn something new for the glory of God.

8. Help someone else for the glory of God.

9. Share your faith with a friend for the glory of God.

10. Obey God's Word for the glory of God.

In all that we do, God wants our hearts and desires to revolve around living for Him. No performance traps. No compartments. No stopping short. God just wants you. Just you.

1. Describe a situation where you were focused on doing something great. _____

_____

_____

2. Describe a time when you felt like you were growing closer to God. Which was more rewarding, growing closer to God or doing something great? _____

_____

_____

3. What is meant by "having a God compartment" in your life? What's so bad about that? _____

_____

_____

4. Create your own top ten list of ways to live for the glory of God. _____

_____

_____

● Check here if you choose to live your life for the glory of God.

CLOSING COMMENT

In the last month, you have made choices about honoring God with your example and your relationships, denying lies, and living right. Here is a summary of the choices we have covered.

- ● iChoose to find creative ways to help others.
- ● iChoose to lead with compassion.
- ● iChoose to do the right thing when nobody's looking.
- ● iChoose to step out with courage.
- ● iChoose to be a careful leader.
- ● iChoose to invest in balanced relationships.
- ● iChoose to honor my parents.
- ● iChoose to be choosy about my friends.
- ● iChoose to save sex for marriage.
- ● iChoose to protect my purity.
- ● iChoose to not do what everyone else is doing.
- ● iChoose to change now and not later.
- ● iChoose to quit believing "I can't."
- ● iChoose to have fun within boundaries.
- ● iChoose to trust in Jesus.
- ● iChoose to be prepared for spiritual battle.
- ● iChoose to use only words that are wholesome, helpful, and beneficial.
- ● iChoose to live my life for an audience of One.
- ● iChoose to get in the game and share my faith.
- ● iChoose to live my life for the glory of God.

Live out your choices in the everyday decisions of real life.